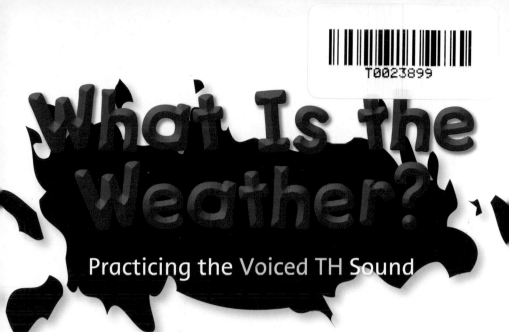

What Is the Weather?

Practicing the Voiced TH Sound

Ethan Lewis

Rosen
PHONICS
READERS

Rosen
Classroom™

It is Father's Day.

My mother and I plan a party.

What will the weather be?

I listen to the weatherman.
The weatherman says
it may rain.

That would be bad!
The party is outside.

My mother says
the weather might change.

Could the weather be sunny?

People gather in our yard.
My father is happy.

There are clouds.
This is not good!

The rain starts.
People gather in the house.

The rain stops.
The weatherman was wrong!

The sun comes out.
The weather is always changing!